Sales Ain't That Damn Hard!

How to Turn Selling into a Fun Conversation

VELECIA L. WILLIAMS

Copyright © 2021 Velecia L. Williams

All rights reserved.

This book or any portion thereof may not be reproduced or used in any manner whatsoever without the expressed written permission of the publisher expect for the use of brief quotations in a book review. Edited by Dawn Burkes. Book Cover & Format by SRJ Business Solutions LLC.

Printed in the United States of America

ISBN: 979-8-599-92442-5

Independently Published by

Velecia L. Williams Publishing LLC

DEDICATION

I would like to dedicate this book to my family and best friends.

Table of Contents

ACKNOWLEDGMENTS I

FOREWORD 1

INTRODUCTION 5

CHAPTER 1: DATE THEM TO SELL THEM 8
- Check Their Social Media 9
- Call Them And Stroke Their Ego 10
- No One-Night Stands 11
- The Check-In Text 11

CHAPTER 2: DRESS FOR THE KILL 14
- What Not To Wear 15
- Be Photoshoot-Ready 18
- Do Your 'Doo 20
- All About The Shoes 22
- Fake It Until You Make It 23

CHAPTER 3: THE FIRST DATE 27
- Be Personable 27
- Mesmerize To Monetize 28
- The Cheese Gets The Cheddar 29
- Spark The Conversation 30

CHAPTER 4: NEVER LEAVE HOME WITHOUT THESE 33
- The Calling Card 34
- Calendar Or Journal For Planning 36
- Pen and pad 37
- Display Your Business 38

CHAPTER 5: EDIFICATION IS EVERYTHING 41
- What Is Edification? 42
- How To Edify: Be Excited About Your Product 43

CHAPTER 6: THE ONE-ON-ONE MEETING 48
- PREQUALIFY: IT'S NOT FOR EVERYONE 49
- BE IN A QUIET PLACE 50
- BE #1 50
- I GOT THIS! 51
- SHOW ME THE MONEY!!! 52

CHAPTER 7: THE DRIP 55
- WHEN TO FOLLOW UP 56
- DRIP UNTIL THEY DIE 57
- KEEP TRACK OF PEOPLE 59
- CHECK SOCIAL MEDIA 59
- ASK FOR THE MONEY AGAIN 61

CONCLUSION 63

APPENDIX: HELPFUL SCRIPTS, TEXTS, & BLANK WORKSHEETS...65
- SO WHAT DO I SAY? - QUICK FUN TEXT SCRIPTS..................................66
- GOAL(S) FOR THE DAY 69
- JOURNAL YOUR DAY 70
- CONTACT LOG..71

ABOUT THE AUTHOR 73

ACKNOWLEDGMENTS

To the love of my life Kiley Marco Williams: You put up with my smoke, my nerves, my tears and my anxiety throughout this project. Losing my father-in-law hurt me deeply. I know I seem to be the strong one, but I am not. I hurt. I know he's your father, but he has a piece of my heart. I caught writer's block during his passing. I told him that I was writing a book and I can still hear him say, "Well, go on, girl!" Thank you for introducing me to your parents. Our relationship is the best of all three marriages ... haha!

To my mother, my loudest cheerleader: Whether you are on the sidelines at my games, sitting in the living room or bragging to your sorors and family, I appreciate you pushing me. The culture and life experiences to which you exposed me made me a strong dynamic replica of you; I got it all from my momma - Earnestine, Miss Tina, Lady E.

To my BFF, Tarra "Madam Money®, DUALpreneur®, SRJ Websites" Jackson. My Oprah, who swears that she is the boss of me - I can't tell you how much it means to have a friend and sister like you. Since you looked me in the face and introduced yourself using your whole, entire name (me 14- and you 15-years-old), I knew that we were going to be peas in a pod (so did our parents). I thank you for working closely with me on this project and more to come. Like you said, "We have too much money to make." I am ready.

Next, my baby Faith: Thank you for your continued gratitude and support. I love you for loving your imperfect mother unconditionally. Whether others want to believe it, I have always done my best for my children. It fills my heart with joy that you notice the hard work and sacrifice it took to get where we are as a family. Your love and support will never be unnoticed. You are smart, beautiful and talented. I am looking forward to your producing and directing one of my books one day.

Last but not least, I also dedicated this to my business partners. Not just the loyal and independent thinker. Each of you are unique in your own way. I speak of perseverance and prosperity over your lives and the lives of your loved ones.

Those listed below believed in my vision before I actually put it to paper. They pushed and cheered for me. Not only that, but they also purchased the book when I only had a book cover. Please take a moment to visit and patronize my friends and colleagues on the next few pages. I love you all.

Marco Williams, 5 Star Limo and Sedan

www.5starlimosc.com

Tarra Jackson, Madam Money

www.madammoney.com

Marty Fort, Columbia Arts Academy

www.columbiaartsacademy.com | **Irmo Arts Academy**, *www.irmomusicacademy.com* | **Lexington Arts Academy,** *www.lexingtonschoolofmusic.com*

Michael Miller, Texas

Marvin Conkley, South Carolina

La'Quita Simmons, Classy Queen Printing FB: @ClassyQueenPrinting

Ursula Jennings, Styled by Ursula FB: @styledbyursula & IG: @styledbyursula

April Colley, The Authoress IG: @therealauthoress

Tennille Lott, Virgin Hair Candy ATL LLC FB: @virginhaircandy

Jassy McBride, McB Travel Services Atlanta *www.Mcbtravel.net*

Dr Philiphia Minor, Vallejo, California

Leah Celeste, The Alora Agency LLC *www.thealoraagency.com*

Angelia Peete, Boss Chics, IG: @b0ss_chic

Nikki Jones, Wilmington, Delaware

Tasha Moore, Toddler Talk Consultants and Training LLC *www.linktr.ee/toddlertalkllc*

Kayla Shekia, Shek Luxe Studio LLC *www.linktr.ee/Kaylashekia*

Dr Shaquana Cuttino Jones, Cuttino Law Firm

www.cuttinolawfirm.com

Glen Scales, Atlanta, Georgia

Deerick Carr, Carr Commercial Cleaning

www.carrcommercialcleaningsvc.com

Faith Alexander, Faith Reniya

www.linktr.ee/faithreniya

Chante Purnell Charles, Chante Purnell Charles LLC *www.linktr.ee/chante_purnellcharles*

Melissa Carassco, East Bay Virtual Services LLC

www.eastbayvirtualservices.com

Damon Hughes, Harrington, Delaware

Dennis and Tizzy Petersen, Stafford, Virginia

Samuel Edith Elzie, LZ & Associates

www.lzhomesales.com

Atty James Boyd, J and J Associates

www.jandjassociates.com

Donald Latimore, The Latimore Team

www.latimore.com

Dawn Burkes, L.A. Times Multiplatform Editor

www.linkedin.com/in/dawnmburkes

With lots of love,

Velecia L Williams

FOREWORD

Sales gets a bad rap. For a lot of people, it's a bad word -- it has negative connotations.

But if you're going to run or work for a successful business, you have to realize that sales is everything.

That's not an overstatement. Any business can have systems. Any business can have services. You can have a business with fantastic systems but low sales, and it will not succeed. You can have a business with superb service but no sales process, and it will fail.

So, sales really is EVERYTHING.

This book aims to help you become better at sales, either as the owner of a small business or the employee of a business.

It starts with the mindset that sales is everything. You have to view sales as a positive and powerful force, not drudgery or something lame. What Velecia is going to show you in this book is that sales really can be FUN if you get in rhythm with it.

The next step is to understand the scope of selling. It's not just being a used car salesman or telemarketer.

Sales is multidimensional.

It's how clean the bathrooms are at your business. It's how clean the plates are in your restaurant. It's the trash picked up from your parking lot. It's the grass cut in front of your office.

Sales is any interaction between you and your customers.

And if you improve your sales process, if you improve your selling abilities, you will have or be a part of a more profitable business (and quickly).

Velecia lays out, and I agree that sales is not hard. With practice, it can become second nature. And the only way to sell on a high level is to make it easy.

Sales is how you dress, how you speak, how you carry yourself. Its mastery is the fastest way to get ahead in business and life.

I wish they would require every middle and high school student to have sales courses. If they did that, we would have a stronger economy and society.

Churches need sales. Hospitals need sales. Charities need sales, and YOU need sales for whatever it is that you do.

I had a friend that said, "I hate selling." I said, "Well, you better hire someone that likes it!"

And that's what this book will help you do.

It will help you enjoy sales, become more of a natural with it, and be more effective as a salesperson.

So, get a highlighter out and read this book twice.

This is your road map to success.

This is the day you can take the first step on your path to making more money for yourself and your family.

And this last part is vital. Do not ever be ashamed of wanting to make money. Many will try to make you feel ashamed for it.

But not me.

Embrace it.

Love money and it will love you back.

Friends come and go, but money gives you the power to do what you want to do in this short life.

So, read this book quickly. Then read it again. Put it into action and get me a sale!

Marty Fort
CEO, Music Academy Success®
Author of the #1 Amazon Best-selling Book, *"The Ultimate Guide to Music Lessons"*

INTRODUCTION

I wrote this book because people make sales complicated. Sales is not that damn hard: It's all in the projection of your product or service. If you're excited about it, if you know the different steps -- how to present and represent yourself or what to do for the first initial contact and what to do during the connection -- it's not that hard.

Sales is a conversation. Grown people have conversations every day: We talk about different things all the time. If you have a favorite food, you talk about that. If you have a favorite movie, you talk about that. What you are doing is selling and marketing that food or that movie. Have you ever looked at social media and someone says something about a restaurant? That is sales. They have sold you on going to that restaurant to eat that dish.

So, it's not that damn hard. All you have to do is relax, have a conversation and close the deal. A lot of people say, *"Work your business."* But do they know how to work their own? Working your business simply means to sell your product and service. I can show you what that means. Let's go ahead and get into the conversation steps to close in sales.

After each chapter, you will find pages for notes as well as a few pages to journal. You will be able to purchase later. But this first set before chapter one is strictly about you. Write your long-term goals and five affirmations to uplift you daily. Positive thoughts give positive results. Remember that the universe is listening and what you tell yourself is true. What anyone else says about you is not your business if it is not positive. I want you to get into the habit of writing your goals for the day. These are called short term goals. Also, get into the habit of logging who you spoke to, how you communicated, what was the outcome, and a date for follow up. The follow up is the deposit slip to your bank account. These practices will help you develop meaningful habits and make it easier for you to have a conversation. I started these habits when I worked for the largest beverage company in the world. This company trains and develops the best salespeople since my silent stock sales mentor. You will figure who these people out once you read this and get to know me more.

CHAPTER 1: Date Them To Sell Them

Get to know a customer before selling them a product or service. My husband hates when I say I date my clients because he says it seems a little sketchy and that I'm trying to flirt to get their attention. But I date them because I want to build a relationship. Relationship-building is important. If you don't have a relationship with your prospect, you're not going to close the deal.

Make sure you leave a lasting impression. Hopefully, when you meet someone, you do due diligence to make sure that they are a fit for you. You want to mesh, something like a physical attraction or characteristic fit. Inspect them and research them. As a wise man said, *"All money ain't good money,"* which means that every customer is not a good fit. It can cost you more money to get with them than getting with them can make. In the sales world, we call them chargebacks or time-wasting creatures.

I did this when I was dating. Prospects must be worthy of your call. Yes! I said, "worthy." Talking to you is a privilege. You have something they need. Make them feel that they can't stop thinking about you and what you said. Keep their wheels turning, especially in the middle of the night. Have you ever had that happen to you? Follow the steps I will outline later to turn a "no" or "not right now" into a yes later.

Check Their Social Media

Check the client's social media to find things that are attractive to them. Let's say you're in real estate and they're looking to buy a home. Do they have children? Do they own a boat? Find things that they like to do so you can have a conversation about those things. Look for their profession to figure out something that they wouldn't need. If they feel like their budget is $200,000 and I'm looking at their profile and see they can't afford something like that, I'll try to steer them in a different way.

LinkedIn and Facebook are good sources. Don't look too much at Instagram or Snapchat because many people put on airs or fake it to make it.

Call Them And Stroke Their Ego

Before you go on a date, you call the person and make them feel good about themselves. So, the guy is 6-4. He's handsome. He has a nice car. He has pretty teeth or whatever you feel is attractive. You call and say, *"Look, I would love to see you driving in your beautiful BMW and meeting me at Tanera Bridge."* The call will turn them on, and they're going to remember you.

It's almost as if it's an interview, and you say, *"You have on a nice shirt today."* I have done that in an interview and gotten the job because interviewing me felt good after I stroked the ego. The shirt was pink. It wasn't nice. It didn't look good, but the interviewer didn't need to know that. What they remembered was that I was personable and complimentary. Flattery gets you everywhere!

That's just how you win someone's attention and reel them into what you have to say.

No One-Night Stands

When you build a relationship with a prospect, the prospect will be there to have a conversation so that you could sell them a product or service. At the end of the conversation and the meeting, you don't want to have them lingering on thinking, *"Well, am I a good fit? Are we going to see each other again? Are we going to do business?"* You want to leave them with a burning need to talk to you; you want them to keep thinking about it.

Please do not text first. If they don't answer, leave a quick message: *"I was just thinking about our conversation."* That's the first call -- in the daytime -- and thank them for taking the time to speak with you. Tell them that you value their time and attention. That makes the prospect know you took the time to listen and that you care. That's called follow-up. Do it quickly.

The Check-In Text

If you're not able to get the prospect on the phone, you want to check in with them by at least sending a text. Always send a follow-up text after a call or meeting. Again, texting is not your first source of communication; it's the second choice. There are so many scam texts that people ignore business text messages even after calling and leaving a voicemail. Many people don't check voicemails, or their voicemails are not working, so a check-in text works better. Doesn't it annoy you when you hear that someone's mailbox is full or not set up? Hell, that's when you will definitely get a text from me.

The check-in text is, *"Hello. How are you? I just called to check in and let you know that I was thinking about our meeting, and I definitely want to do business with you. I think that the product or service that I have will add value to what you're doing."* The check-in text should be fewer than 115 words. It doesn't matter which messaging platform you use but remember to pay attention to the received message signals. All platforms have them. Remember to reference them, thank them and let them know that you are looking forward to meeting them again. End the message with an emoji. Scammers don't use emojis.

NOTES

CHAPTER 2: Dress For The Kill

First impressions are lasting impressions. When you walk into a room, you want people to remember you for your professional look. You don't want to leave the impression that you don't have it together. Let's talk about clothes, including makeup, hair and accessories for men and women. In this chapter, I don't want to focus on women.

These things are important because when you walk across that space to give a presentation, people will remember you. When you walk into the room to sit down with someone, people are going to remember you. You don't even have to start your conversation, and you won't have a conversation that someone can focus on if you don't dress for the kill.

What Not To Wear

For men

Men are always left out of some topics when a woman explains it. If you're a salesperson, you've heard that *"the first impression is the last impression."* You come in with a tie, a dark suit, a nice white shirt, some nice shoes and a watch. Men don't have too many accessories, so that the watch can become a conversation piece. If you coordinate everything well, you will make a lasting impression on the person with which you're sitting. What you're wearing will help start the conversation, and it will help you build a relationship. Remember, this whole thing is about building relationships.

So, come in suited-up, nice and tailored. I would not recommend skinny pants or jeans, though that depends on where you're located. If you're in Europe, Italian suits will work. In the United States, a regular suit is good, and it doesn't have to cost that much; go to a department store and pick something off the rack if you choose. Tailor-made suits are for when you start making lots of dollars. No earrings. Make sure you're clean-cut, including beard and eyebrows. Incredible Hulk eyebrows are not a good look. Make sure people like what they see and that they won't exclaim, *"What in the world is wrong with their eyebrows?"*

When women see men wear nice shoes, it becomes a conversation piece. Ties are not always mandatory. Ladies, have you ever seen a man in a nice suit with a partially open button-up shirt? Yes! Keep my attention. These suggestions depend on the product, service and situation. Plan accordingly and look your absolute best!

For women

"What Not to Wear" is a touchy topic for women. Someone once asked me, *"What are you selling?"* It was insulting because this lady didn't know how to dress even though she was making more money than I was. She told me one time that I looked as if I was selling more than travel. At first, I was offended, but then I looked at the source.

And this is what I picked out of that statement: One, my dress was fitted. Two, my shoes were stiletto heels. Three, my accessories were a little bulky. Four, my makeup was not heavy, and five, I have long hair. Now, she looked like an old hag to me.

My definition of an old hag and your definition of an old hag may be different. The person that I am speaking of couldn't coordinate two plaid patterns together if they matched. She wore her hair in a mushroom and had on pale makeup; she was not the best person to give advice on how a salesperson should look. I am more of a modern-dressed professional, and she is more of a professionally dressed nanny from a famous movie. I digress.

In sales, a big, sloppy suit is not a nice look. Your clothes should always fit. If you're buying off the rack, you should always get the size tailored to fit. I'm not saying to make it tight so that your skirt or dress will rise. But you shouldn't wear anything with lots of loose parts. That goes for men and women.

Jewelry should not be bulky when you're going to a sales meeting, but it's acceptable for a sales presentation because you want all eyes on you. In the sales conversation, you want them to focus on the conversation and not on what you're wearing. Heels at least two inches high are a must for me, but I don't wear a platform shoe when I am going to a business meeting.

I worked for a beverage company when I lived in California, and I think I was the only woman in my market who wore heels and a nice outfit to visit a client. I made a lasting impression, and I also made outstanding numbers.

I did not want to look like I was one of the merchandisers. I wanted to make sure that I look like a saleswoman. And yes, I did walk to my territory in a heel. I walked in, and I talked to the client and I looked very professional at all times.

That's what you want to do; you always want to look professional. You can step out of the box just a bit when you're doing a presentation but be professional.

Be Photoshoot-Ready

For women

Makeup and accessories are essential. In your sales presentation, you may go a little bold with your accessories. But when you're sitting down in front of someone, your accessories need to calm down. Pearls work great for those occasions. In my real estate business, I have on pearls when I see clients. When I meet them at open houses, I have pearls: small pearl earrings and a little pearl necklace or a drop necklace. I do not wear anything other than pearls, and I hope to influence others to do the same.

Do you know why I wear pearls? It makes me feel royal. It makes me feel as if I am going to dominate the sale. It gives me confidence because I feel like I'm a queen. All women should feel like they're queens. Wear your pearls or wear light jewelry.

Your makeup is your MAKE UP. Keep eyebrows natural-looking. The "brown eyebrows" and "Instagram eyebrows" are very distracting. When you're sitting in front of your client or giving a presentation, your eyebrows should not be overwhelming. Unless you're going to a party or a photo shoot, keep your lashes natural. It's OK! Looking like a "Sesame Street" character doesn't look professional unless you're selling makeup. Even then, it can be overbearing.

Believe it or not, thick, long eyelashes are a trend that is quickly turning into a stereotype; many people feel the lashes are ridiculous and don't fit into the law of attraction. If you don't believe me, ask ten professionals (not your peers). You want all eyes on you, but you don't want your eyes to be a view. I just want to make sure that you close the sale and attract a client to build a relationship, not distract them.

Once, I posted a picture on Facebook of a young lady picking up food for a famous delivery company. She was wearing clogs, basketball shorts, a dusty-looking T-shirt and a scarf. Her car was filthy. One of my "friends" messaged me and asked, "What's wrong with that? Did she have to dress up just to deliver food? She is a regular person." Now, before I responded, I tried to see what she was thinking. So, I broke it down like this: *"I am regular. Do you see me posting name brands? Yes, she is delivering food, but she represents a company. Someone's prepared food is riding in a dirty car. It won't hurt her to put on a polo shirt or red T-shirt with a pair of pants and sneakers or shoes. I am sure she has that around the house. It won't hurt her to clean her car, either. That doesn't count?"* She never replied, but I know she knew what the hell I said. It takes a little effort to make lots of dollars. You can't say that the struggle is real when you are the struggle.

Do Your 'Doo

For women

For your sales presentation, your hair should be simple. I love long hair, and nowadays everybody wears long hair with most of it as extensions. So, keep it simple. If you're going to wear your hair, don't have it really big. Don't have it in a bright color, unless you're in fashion.

In some places, the culture can be different. When it comes to hair and makeup and accessories, they either don't care or care. There is a culture that affirms blue hair. There's a culture that doesn't mind red hair. But, in my opinion, blue hair or red hair does not close the deal.

Many people like to say your personality is your accessory and it makes you who you are. Or, that it's your knowledge that makes you who you are and that's what closes the deal. They like to say your hair does not make you who you are.

I beg to differ.

When you walk into the room to give a presentation, you want all eyes on you and not a big view. You're not a monument. You're not a presentation of fireworks. You could get fireworks in your personality but not red hair or big hair. Blonde hair is OK, but keep it toned down (and you know who I am talking to). You can also tone down the curls. No big hair, no big curls. Dreadlocks are okay, but they have to be neat, tapered and brown or naturally colored. This is because Corporate America kind of frowns on dreadlocks anyway, so you don't want to make it a big issue. No matter how you style your hair, you don't want it all over the place, with a color that isn't natural.

For men

If you are wearing an afro, make sure it's low-cut and tapered. Men should not have a whole lot of oil in their hair; you'll look like a greaser. Remember "Grease"? They call those guys greasers. You shouldn't have that.

All About The Shoes

For women

Have you ever watched somebody look at you? Did you notice that they start from the bottom and then go up? It's a couple of things they're looking for, and the first one is your shoes. If your shoes are messy, your personality is messy, and you don't care. That means you're not going to deliver the type of service that a client wants.

It's like a messy car. Some people say you can tell a lot about a person by how a person keeps their car. It's the same with the shoes. I am particular when it comes to shoes and especially in the sales profession. Red shoes are not permitted. I learned that in banking from a write-up. Black or brown or dark gray shoes should suffice. When I worked in the beverage industry, I always wore black shoes because I was always in front of a client.

For men

The same thing goes for men. I know you like your snakeskin loafers with the velvet and all that good stuff, but that does not pertain to sales. Keep the velvet and pointed shoes for when you go out. They're nice, but they're not for sales; keep a round, oval or a square toe. There should be nothing too flashy -- no sparkles, glitter or gold. Just keep it simple.

Fake It Until You Make It

You don't have to spend your whole paycheck on an outfit just to impress your client. Know your pace. Know what you can genuinely afford. There are plenty of websites and stores that offer nice, affordable clothes and accessories. Everything doesn't have to be a name brand. Google your favorite style and look for it piece by piece and pay a fraction of the cost for something similar. Millionaires do it all the time. But if you must have name brands, look to consignment shops and Goodwill stores in wealthy neighborhoods.

Fake it until you make it.

A friend needed a suit for an interview. I went to a Goodwill in Roswell, Georgia, in the Atlanta metropolitan area and found a nice suit, jacket and slacks in navy blue, for $20. I also found a tie and a handkerchief, but I don't recommend that part; it just came together. I also found a nice white shirt for him. All of this was brand-name. So, you can go to a thrift store and find something nice; just take it to the cleaners. This suit and the whole outfit probably valued at $500. You don't have to spend that much money on your clothes.

Fake it until you make it.

There are department stores that have name-brand clothes, including economically priced nice suits and dresses. I've paid as little as $4 for an item. You don't have to spend more than $20 on shoes.

Now, some of you are probably reading this and saying, *"You know what? She's probably a knock-off queen. She probably wears cheaply made clothes."* But I don't. I'm a sales rep, so I have a lot of shoes and clothes. That's not because I went out and spent a lot of money. You don't have to pay a lot of money to look like a million dollars.

My mother always told me that you don't have to look like what you're going through. So, if you are broke, so what? Your client doesn't know you're broke. Your client sees somebody that is clean-cut. Your client sees someone who dresses well, who speaks well, and who wants to do business. Be clean-cut and dapper: GQ for the men and Modern Style for the women. You can look like you're coming out of a magazine, but you don't have to spend that type of money.

NOTES

CHAPTER 3: The First Date

The first date/meeting is crucial when it comes to face-to-face sales. This is the initial impression of how you're going to present your product or service. Let's talk about being personable, looking into a client's eyes, always smiling and sparking the conversation. This first date is going to allow you to get to know them and start building a relationship. They will want to move forward with you in whatever you're selling. It's going to help you in the long run, as well as in the present. The first date is the beginning of your future.

Be Personable

What's being personable? The conversation is always about them, not about you. You want to compliment them and, of course, you've already done your research. So, anything that you present should match your research. Because I am in network marketing and real estate, I have coached people in being personable because that's the way you build your relationship: Use what you know about them, their family, what you want to know about their occupation. You want to know about things they do in their spare time, and you also want to know what they do for a living.

When you use those things to be personable, you will touch their soft spots. You want to make sure the prospect knows everything you're talking about is about them. Always keep them in the forefront of your conversation when you're trying to close them. That's a lasting impression.

Mesmerize To Monetize

It's important to look into your client's eyes. Have you ever heard someone say that the eyes have it or the eyes tell it all? That is true; your eyes can say everything. I have a problem sometimes using my eyes while I'm talking. My eyes give away my emotions, whether I'm upset, happy, excited. When you look into a client's eyes, they will tell you whether the client is interested, impressed, or even want to talk to you again. Stare into their eyes to see what they're thinking. Their eyes have it. I bet you didn't know that their voice represents their eyes as well, did you? It's the tone. Look into that. Do you see it?

The Cheese Gets The Cheddar

You are not fully dressed without a smile. Smiling is essential in a meeting because you want to let the client know that you're happy about sitting with them, you enjoy their conversation and that your product or service is exciting. It says a lot about the character of a person who doesn't look into somebody's eyes and smile. Character is everything.

People say that I have a habitual smile. If I'm having a bad day, the client doesn't need to know. If I'm having a good day, the client needs to know. Every day is a good day when you open your eyes. So, when you see me, you're always going to see a smile, and that's what you should always do because your smile says a lot about you. Especially if you have nice teeth, your smile says that you have everything together.

Spark The Conversation

Know what you are talking about. You want the client to feel comfortable deciding to work with you. Stay in control of the call. Don't let them out-script you. That means that you are the expert. You want them to use your product or your service. It's your business to make them feel like they're missing out if they don't have what you have to offer.

Please don't get commission breath: no begging, no convincing. So, when you're sparking the conversation, you have already been personable. You've already complimented the client, but you want to spark this conversation just by saying a few words like, *"Hey, how was your day today? Are you having a great day?"* Ask some open-ended questions that will get them to loosen up because you're building a relationship.

So, when I spark a conversation, I begin by saying, *"How are you? It's been a long time since we've spoken."* I continue the conversation: *"What's going on with you? Are you traveling? What are you doing today? What are you doing in your life right about now?"* They'll respond because you sought the conversation. Then you talk to them about your product or service.

If you take the first step, they will follow you to the final step. Start the conversation. Tell them about your product or service. In return, they will follow through.

NOTES

CHAPTER 4: Never Leave Home Without These

Take your tools when you're going to a sales event, even if you're just sitting in front of a client. The tools that you need include business cards, a planning calendar, and a pen and pad with your logo on them. You also want to have some statistics. OK, I have gone to a meeting and I didn't have my business cards. And a lot of people will say, *"Do you have a business card?"* I don't really like paper and clutter. So, I keep my business card accessible on my cell phone so that I can share my information. Displaying your business is essential when you're in sales because you want someone to feel like they're missing out if they don't have your product or service.

Your calendar says a lot about what you do. If you have empty spaces on your calendar, then that means you're not doing any business. You don't have any appointments to set. If you don't have any appointments set, you don't have any sales and you're not making any money.

It's important to have your calendar ready when you're ready to do business. Within that calendar, you should have your database. I have learned that your database -- your clients and potential clients -- is your data bank. That's why setting up your calendar is so important. It's your ATM card. You can't withdraw what you don't deposit.

The Calling Card

Business cards are essential for business, though I recommend going digital. I have used digital cards since I first took a picture of a business card with my smartphone.

It wasn't in my budget to buy cards when I started my first business. The company only provided me with 10 cards on which I had to write my name. (Those were the days.) I would take a picture of my card and text or email it instead of handing out cards. I didn't know that I was ahead of the game with building my database!

Have you ever been somewhere, and you've given out all of your business cards? Or what if you were somewhere sparking a conversation, then turn around to see one of your cards on the floor? So, you may have spent $100 on 500 cards (probably more if you didn't use an online service). That card on the floor will make you feel unimportant and that you missed an opportunity to get the person's information because you only passed out a card. You're not a flyer person or a promoter. That's why I believe in digital. I want to reciprocate the contact information. I'll text or email you my card. At that point, I have your email address. I have your phone number. Then, later on, I could text or call you to start our dating process. Plus, you will have my information. After that point, if you want to block me, that's fine, but you have my information for future reference.

I'm in the travel and real estate industries. I use an app through which I can send my card or contact information. A client can also download the app and get my contact information; the app will send a link and my business and card will pull up.

When I took a picture of my business card with my phone, the card's quality wasn't right. So, I downloaded images of the card's front and back to my phone into a separate folder. That way, the card was readily available. The text message I sent with the card would say, *"Thank you for speaking with me today. I know we'll get together another time."* Now, they have my information, and they can refer to a greeting to spark the conversation and set the appointment after that.

If you would like access to some of the tools that I use, go to www.salesaintthatdamhard.com/tools. You can find details on some of the things that I use to stay in touch with prospects, including the app that I use.

Calendar Or Journal For Planning

Use a calendar to stay organized. Do not keep your personal life and your business life together.

Stay organized so you won't overbook. You can use an online calendar to have two calendars in one. Using a journal and a digital calendar keeps you much more organized with life; you have to have balance.

You can find a calendar journal that caters to this need at *www.salesaintthatdamnhard.com/tools.* The digital calendar can set reminders for you. My digital calendar starts my day with an alarm. I set reminders for the day before, an hour earlier, 30 minutes earlier, 15 minutes earlier, and 10 minutes before I have an appointment or an event. I want to keep a constant reminder so that if I need to do some research the day before, I can get that done and cross that off my to-do list in my journal.

My journal calendar contains my to-do list or what I did for the day and what I spoke with the client about, then I can set a date to follow up. It's basically an affordable Customer Management Tool. I highly recommend that you have both of these items: The digital one will keep you on schedule. The journal is to ensure that you have followed up, done everything on your to-do list, and can brain-dump for the next day. Brain-dumping is crucial because you don't want to take your work to bed with you and have sleepless nights.

Pen and pad

It's important to be prepared. You definitely want to have a pen and pad. Take notes at all times but maintain eye contact with the customer. I don't know if you remember shorthand. But my mom used it all the time. It looked like a group of symbols. You could make your own shorthand by writing keywords and critical points that you and the client speak about so that you can have it for the next conversation.

You don't want to go to a meeting without a pen and pad because you'll be unprepared. It's just like going to school. You never went to school without a pen and pad because you were there to learn. You are in front of the client to discover who they are and their reaction to your product or service.

Display Your Business

Create a social media page for your business. Make sure you have that information so that when people are looking for a specific product or service, your business or service is on display for them to connect with you. People follow you because they want to know all about you. They want to see if you actually are traveling, if you're actually selling lotions, if you're actually selling makeup. Be a product of your product, always.

Potential customers want to know what you're doing with your product or service that you have and if you're using it. A lot of times, people will say they're doing something and not doing it. But social media would display that.

If you're a vendor at an event or speaking at an event, you should have a banner. If it's an event for a company, ask the event planner beforehand if you can bring the banner out because it will help tell your story. My banner has my contact information, including my name, website and phone number.

Attendees can take a picture of the banner, use it as a reference and later reach out to you. As a vendor, you should have a table with a tablecloth with your logo or your name. Don't forget social media information on your displays, which should be your business page, Instagram page and even

Snapchat and your LinkedIn information. Become your marketing and advertising company. Display daily. Your cash flow depends on it.

NOTES

CHAPTER 5: Edification Is Everything

First, let me define the word edify. According to Merriam Webster, to edify is "to instruct or improve (someone) morally or intellectually."

Edification is so important when it comes to sales. We will talk about how we teach about products and services, being excited and telling the story about them. You want to make the customer feel as if they can't function without the product or service. You want to leave them thinking about it, then setting up appointments to discuss it. You want to explain your product or service to the point that they will remember you and your product or service when you leave them.

They may watch TV and see something about that same product or service. If it's travel and they see a picture of a popular resort, they're going to think about booking that, and then I can make money. Or maybe you have talked about a detox tea and you were so excited about it that any time they see something like it in a store, they say to themselves, "You know what? I need this tea. I need to detox. Let me call my salesperson or go to their website and get that tea." That's because you have taught them about it. You were excited. You told a story. And you made it so animated that they're going to remember it whenever they see it somewhere else.

What Is Edification?

What is edification and why is it important when it comes to sales? Edification in sales is mainly describing the highlights of your product or service. It shows the value of what you're bringing to the client and it also helps get feedback. You will uplift your product or service by describing it, telling what it is, the history behind it and how it will benefit them.

Introductions are part of edification. It tells their credentials and helps the person on the other end feel as if they are significant. For instance, in network marketing, we use edification. We edify a few things. We enlighten the person, and we illuminate the product. An example of something of value would be who that person is, what their title is, what they have done to get where they are and a fun fact about them and how they're going to help you. The same thing with the product or service: You want to introduce what it is, how it can benefit the client, what's a fun fact about it and how it will help them.

How To Edify: Be Excited About Your Product

Why should someone be excited about their product? Have you ever had someone talk to you about a product or service and you can tell they've never used it before? A lot of times, this happens when people are just starting in their industry. You want to be excited about it and tell a story about it. Being excited about a product can highlight your knowledge of the product.

Let me give you an example of how someone can be excited about their product and use that excitement to close the sale. In network marketing, we do a three-way call. We edify by talking about the product or service we're offering the client in the three-way call. Now when I am talking about a product, I get excited about it because I want the client to get excited. When the client gets off the phone, I want them to say, "Man, that sounds so good that I might want to get into it right now. I have to have it. Let me just go to this website." Your excitement for the product or service is going to excite someone else.

Now, I have had to coach a team member. She was talking about her travel business in a monotone. She wasn't excited. It seems like she was just "doing her business." So, in our coaching time, I said, "Look, when you're in front of the people or you're on the phone with someone, if you're not excited, if you're talking in the tone that you're talking, do you really think that someone's going to purchase from you or someone's going to join your business? And she said, "No. that's what I have you for," because she's speaking about third-party validation. But you are the person who has to pique the interest of the client. You're the person who wants to get them in front of the product or service first because they count on you.

So, if you're not using your product or service, it will definitely show. If you're on social media, be excited about your products. Post all the time: Share stories and posts about what you're doing with the product or service. Keep an eye on the people. All of that shows that you're excited about it. And the more you're excited about it, the more you attract people to your product or service and close more sales.

Have you ever heard the expression that people don't remember the facts, they remember the stories? That's what you should do when you are selling your product or service. You want to remind the customer that they need this product or service, that if they don't have it, they won't be able to function.

For instance, say that you are in real estate and show a client a series of houses. Use the things you know about them if you want to hit their soft point and find it in a home. Make them think if they don't have it that they're not going to be happy. An example: They look at houses and five of them don't have an island. But the last house has one, and the island is something they mentioned in their consultation or their first conversation with you. You're going to say that and tell a story about how the island will benefit their family: big dinners, extra dining space. Make it so they must have this house with the island.

And if it's a service, you want them to think that if they don't have this service, they won't be able to function in their everyday life. So, if you are in the travel industry, travel is your service. We provide that service to friends or family, or people could do that for themselves. And if they're booking trips on other websites and not booking trips on their website, they're not making any money. They're actually throwing away money. You have to tell a story about that. I like to talk about how this one travel company owns every website where you book travel and people don't know that. And when they find out, they're like, "Wow, that's something." And I affirm that by telling them to "Go Google it if you don't believe me."

NOTES

CHAPTER 6: The One-On-One Meeting

Let's talk about the one-on-one meeting, the meat and potatoes of closing your deal. It's not the conclusion; it's from the beginning to the end of the closing. So, we're going to talk about prequalifying, because the meeting is not for everyone—some things you can do over the phone.

If you meet in person, meet the potential customer in a quiet place and have a one-on-one conversation to build a relationship. You don't want distractions. Being there first is very impressionable and allows you to set the scene up for the meeting. And then ask for the money. A lot of times we are afraid to ask for the money. And I'm going to show you how to get closing comments that ask for the money indirectly.

Prequalify: It's Not For Everyone

We've already talked about the first date, but it's important to prequalify. This may not be for everyone. It's like going on a date. Before you jump in a car on the first date, you want to make sure you ask probing questions to make sure you want to go on this date. You want to make sure you want to go to this first meeting with this client.

So, I prequalify a person before I get to the first meeting, I ask probing questions: What are you looking for in a home? Have you looked at your credit lately? If not, do you mind if we pull your credit? What is the time frame for you to close on your home? What are you looking for in a salesperson? Depending on the answers, either keep it as a phone consultation or meet up to start the process.

As with any other industry, everybody's not going to want your product or service. It's good to prequalify a potential customer because they will tell you upfront whether they want it or not. You just have to listen.

Be In A Quiet Place

When you're starting your one-on-one meeting, you must go to a quiet place so that you can listen to your client and your client can listen to you. Pick somewhere intimate like a coffee shop, a sandwich shop or maybe even a wine bar, depending on their personality. If you've done your research, you'll know whether this person likes to drink coffee or if this person is a foodie or doesn't mind a sip of wine.

A quiet place is vital because if there's a lot of noise, it's a distraction. I don't want to have a lot of music and loud noises surrounding me because I can't keep my client's attention. I've already caught their attention, walking in the room and sitting down. So, when we're getting ready to start our conversation, I want all eyes to be on me. They're focused on me. They're not worried about distractions. This is why a quiet place is very, very important.

Be #1

When I was in the marching band in college, my coach used to say, "If you're on time, you're late. If you're late, don't show up." Or "If you're early, you're on time." So, you want to get to any meeting first so you can set up the scene. Set the scene by sending a text to see if they would like a bite to eat or something to drink and let them know that you're already there. And that's a good thing; if you're already there, it tells a lot about you. People don't like a person who will be late because it says they're not important to you. You continue setting up the scene by getting your tools together: Set out your calendar, your pen and paper and your laptop if needed to show a presentation or your flip board, etc. So, when your client walks in, you can stand up, shake their hand and start business.

I Got This!

You must pay the tab. You don't want your client to spend money on the meeting because you're trying to sell them something and want them to spend money with you. That's why you pick a coffee shop or a gourmet sandwich shop, not a McDonald's. That way, if you have to pay out of pocket, it's not going to be a considerable expense.

Remember, it can be a tax write-off because you can file half of that on your taxes. I'm not a tax professional, but if you Google things to write off on your taxes, entertainment is one of them. You are meeting the client at that place and paying for the tab is an entertainment expense.

If you have a company credit card, you can spend more. I worked in Corporate America and had a company card with a limit on what we can spend each day. So, I'll pick the appetizer, spoil my client and pay for the tab.

Show Me The Money!!!

When you're asking for the money, you're actually closing the deal. So, don't be afraid. You want to use closing questions or comments that direct the customer to say yes, such as, "Will we be signing up today?" Or "All I need is a little bit of information to get you started today." If you don't ask for the money, you're not closing the deal, especially if you have a product or service because many products and services have a cost behind them.

Present your product or service as an investment. On taxes or anything like that, give them advice on what they could do to contact their tax professionals so they can write off any startup calls or any products to start that business. A lot of those things are tax-deductible.

When you're closing your deal, don't be afraid to ask for the money. Asking indirectly is the best way to do it.

NOTES

CHAPTER 7: The Drip

What is the drip? The drip is a simple follow-up, staying in contact with your client. We're going to talk about when to follow up, why everyone deserves a call, keeping track of people, checking social media for changes and asking for the money just in case you didn't get it in the beginning.

The drip is just a strategy to keep you in the front of someone's mind when it comes to a product or a service because they may be presented with the same product or service and they'll remember,

"Oh, well, Diane has the same product or service, and she has been in contact with me more. Even though this may be my cousin, she may have more knowledge than my cousin because she has been in contact with me more."

In this chapter, you'll read about strategies for following up with people because there is a system. If you have that system, it will help you close the sale and make more money.

When To Follow Up

My recommendation for following up goes back to Chapter One when I talked about no one-night stand and the check-in text. You want to follow up immediately. You want to thank them for meeting with you. You want to follow up and thank them for coming to your event.

You could do this in a couple of forms. You could text or call. The most popular follow-up communication is by email. If you text or email, you want to follow up with a call. So, don't treat them like a one-night stand. Make that follow-up the first activity that you do.

And then you want to put them on a campaign system because the more people hear your name and your products or service, they're going to be more favorable to buying your products and service and they're going to remember you. There have been times where I hear in my network marketing company that someone has taken and enrolled someone's mother, someone's aunt, someone's customer into their business. And that's because the person that actually got looked over never followed up or spoke to anybody about their business, product and service. I call that body snatching. So, if you don't follow up, somebody's going to snatch the body.

You want to set up a campaign in specific ways. After the first follow-up, you want to follow up with them again. My recommended way: Give them a break after the first day. On the third day, you want to call and check in on them and make them that important. The next week, you want to follow up with them either by email or by text. The following month, you want to follow up with an email, a text and a phone call and just keep doing it week by week until they tell you not to call them anymore. If someone blocks my number, that's not telling me they don't want to talk to me. So, they're going to get either a text from me or an email. I call it drip until they die.

Drip Until They Die

Everyone deserves a call.

We're in an age of technology: People are texting and emailing. A lot of us don't even text or call, preferring email.

I believe that a phone call lends a personal touch. A client should be able to set a date so they can close with you. They shouldn't have to run you down. So if you're calling them constantly as part of the follow-up, they're going to know that you're important to them and you want their business or you want to join their business. You want them to be a part of your service.

Don't get attached to text messaging and email because a lot of times, when we wake up in the morning and there's an email, we look at it, swipe it and delete it. Or we will look at a text and decide that we're going to get back with it. But if someone receives a call, they will more than likely go back and read that text message. That's because they'll feel that person probably has the thing that I need and will answer any questions in a text or email.

I believe everyone deserves a call and that it's the most courteous and the most personal way to keep business and build relationships.

Keep Track Of People

So why do you keep track of people with whom you're following up? Have a system where you can tell whether they're opening your email. Have a system where you can send automatic text messages. Schedule texting and email and call back after the follow-up email. Send thank-you, holiday and birthday cards. If you know that they have a hobby, personalize the pitch: Send them a card in advance so that when National Fishing Day comes, they'll find the card. Comment on some of their posts on social media. If you keep track of them, they will feel like they are important to you and then want to do business with you.

Below is an example of a Contact Log to help you keep track of people for follow up.

Name	Phone	Email	Purpose of Call	Outcome of Call	F/U Date	F/U Time
Jane Doe	*404-555-5555*	*Jane.doe @email.com*	*To discuss relocation & housing needs*	*Wants to buy home in 30 days*	*2/11/19*	*2PM ET*

Check Social Media

Life changes daily. Check social media to see if the prospective customer had a life-changing event. When you're following up with them, you can use the proper dialogue to push their soft spot. Social media has private messaging, and there is an indication of whether that person has looked at your private message. When you send a text message, you don't know whether the person looked at it unless they have an iPhone or have a phone with a messaging app that shows indications. A lot of people don't know how to set those notifications on their phone.

So, check them out on social media. When you're having a conversation about your product or service and want to close them, you will have probed a soft spot to let them know they are important to you.

Other methods of contact

I have NEVER been a huge fan of doing business by text. But in the past couple of years, I have learned that texting is actually better than email! How many times have you received notifications of an email and swiped it from your phone? You have never taken the time to even open it.

Now, whether you answer a text or not, you open it and read it. It doesn't matter who it is from, even if you may suspect it as SPAM. I ran a poll on my social media platforms, and it showed (also in my experience) that texting is a better form of communicating with clients than email! Who knew? I just felt that it was so impersonal. So, in an intro text, send a digital card and reference your social media business page. Watch how many responses you get.

Another method of contact is social media ads. Ask a question that will spark your ideal client or customer's interest and for just $20, you will receive more engagement. Remember, a "like" is a bite, so prey. Your ads on social media can run all at one time using one tool. The object is to automate and condense administrative tasks so you can be out in the field getting more business.

Ask For The Money Again

Keep up with your clients' information! Have a calendar that links to Gmail, a virtual number to keep your business separate from your personal with a dialer app. Send email drips, text drips, automate business and more!

NOTES

CONCLUSION

Congratulations! You have gone through the seven steps of closing a deal. Sales is not that damn hard.

All you have to do is follow these steps, tweaking it to suit your style and taste. Just open up to your client. Smile. Take them on a date. Dress to impress. Be very personable. Do your research on them, and you will definitely close the deal.

We want to make sure that everybody wins no matter what industry. My goal with this book is for the reader to learn how to sell without pressure. Just have fun. Just be excited. Journal your progress. Let's make money. Just do the damn thing.

Need more help? Reach out so I can help work with you on how to earn a significant income in sales. Again, congratulations and like I said, let's do the damn thing.

APPENDIX: Helpful Scripts, Texts, & Blank Worksheets

So What Do I Say? - Quick Fun Text Scripts

No matter what anyone says, scripts work. One of my favorite salesmen of all times that has a movie out that I absolutely love confirmed this. The number one beverage company that I worked for trained me on scripts. Even the brokerage that I have my license with says scripts are necessary. Do I believe them? Damn right. Think about it. A trick or treater had to learn how to walk up to a door and say, "Trick or Treat!" That is a script! If you sat in a training and wrote down something that the instructor or trainer said because you wanted to duplicate what was said, that is a script. A script is simply a footnote of what you are going to say and perfecting it before saying it. How many times have you struggled with what to say? Or how to say it? When to say it? Stick to the script. Make it your own. Practice on someone you do not know and someone you know. Find your biggest hater and practice on them. Then close.

In the book I spoke about connecting with your customer. Remember until you close, you just have a customer. Once you close them, then they become your client. Knowing the difference with this, will help you relax more. Below, you will see a few texts that I have trained sales professionals on. Again, I am not a fan of texting, but since this is the new form of communication, I had to get with it. It is ESPECIALLY important to take your customer quickly from high tech to high touch.

No matter what anyone says, scripts work. One of my favorite salesmen of all times that has a movie out that I absolutely love confirmed this. Even the brokerage that I have my license with says this. Do I believe them? Damn right. Think about it. a trick or treater had to learn how to walk up to a door and say, 'Trick or Treat''. That's a script! It is simply a footnote to what you are going to say and perfecting it.

If you would like to schedule a FREE 15-minute call to discuss any parts of the book, please visit my website at www.velecialwilliams.com.

Icebreaker Texts:

"Hey [name] this is Velecia, hope all is well. I need your help with something. Call me when you get a moment please"

"Hi [name]! I was checking in on you. I know that you are busy, do you have a moment?"

"Hey [name] Hope all is well! Have time for coffee?"

"Haven't seen you in a while [name] :) How about lunch/breakfast/dinner?"

"Thinking of you on this wonderful [day of the week] [name]! Free to talk?"

"Hey [name] It has been a long time since we have had a chance to meet up. I was just checking on you. One day this will all be over. Do you have time to catch up through video chat?"

Goal(s) For The Day

Write one to five personal and sales goals you would like to accomplish for the day. Be sure to make them S.M.A.R.T. (Specific, Measurable, Attainable, Realistic, and Time-Driven)

_____
_____
_____
_____
_____
_____
_____
_____
_____
_____
_____
_____
_____
_____

VELECIA L. WILLIAMS

Journal Your Day

Get in the habit of making time every day to journal about your day. Journaling is best with a pen and paper, however typing in a document or app is good if you like technology. Here are few prompts to help you get started.

- *What clients did you meet with today?*
- *How did the meeting go & when will you follow up?*
- *What did you learn today?*
- *Who did you help today?*

_____

_____

_____

_____

_____

_____

_____

VELECIA L. WILLIAMS

Contact Log

Create a spreadsheet to keep track of prospects and customers. Here is an example of a Contact Log you can use to help you follow up.

Name	Phone	Email	Purpose of Call	Outcome of Call	F/U Date	F/U Time
Jane Doe	404-555-5555	Jane.doe@email.com	To discuss relocation & housing needs	Wants to buy home in 30 days	2/11/19	2PM ET

VELECIA L. WILLIAMS

ABOUT THE AUTHOR

Velecia L Williams is a wife and mother of three. She is a native of Dover, DE and relocated to Atlanta, GA (the "mecca of the south") in 1998. Soon after her migration to Atlanta, she started a home-based business.

However, she was not serious about being an entrepreneur because of her fear of SALES.

In 2012, she took a leap of faith and moved to San Francisco, California. After working long hours at her job, getting overlooked for promotions, and suffering through a daily four-hour commute, she decided to take another stab at owning her own business.

With a great deal persistence, consistency and drive, Velecia mastered the Art of Sales and is now a successful full time business owner! Her mission now is to help other overcome their fear of Sales to attain the revenue and lifestyle they desire and deserve.

Whether in front of thousands or in a living room with a small group, Velecia speaks with passion and enthusiasm helping thousands reach their entrepreneurial goals.

To learn more about, work with or book Velecia L. Williams to speak, visit *www.velecialwilliams.com*.

VELECIA L. WILLIAMS

www.ingramcontent.com/pod-product-compliance
Lightning Source LLC
Chambersburg PA
CBHW071420210526
45465CB00001B/469